USA FOR AFRICA

GILDA BERGER

USA
FOR
AFRICA

ROCK AID
IN THE
EIGHTIES

FRANKLIN WATTS | 1987
NEW YORK | LONDON | TORONTO | SYDNEY

Frontis: *a panoramic view of the Live Aid concert in JFK Stadium in Philadelphia. Inset: malnourished mother and child at a refugee camp in Ethiopia*

Photographs courtesy of UPI/Bettmann Newsphotos: pp. 2, 58, 71, 72, 80, 86, 87, 88; Care Photo by Rudolph von Bernuth: pp. 2 (inset), 24, 27, 28, 29 (top and bottom left), 30, 36; Columbia Records: p. 13; RCA Records and Tapes: p. 14; David Redfern/Retna Ltd.: pp. 15 (left), 16, 17, 18; Gary Gershoff/Retna Ltd.: pp. 15 (right), 21 (top), 73 (bottom), 75, 81 (top); Darlene Hammond/Retna Ltd.: pp. 21 (bottom left), 47; Michael Putland/Retna Ltd.: 32, 73 (top); Care Photo: p. 29 (bottom right); Tritec Music Limited 1984: p. 34; Chip E./Retna Ltd.: p. 35; John Bellissimo/Retna Ltd.: pp. 38, 60 (right), 78; Chris Walter/Retna Ltd.: p. 41; Robin Kaplan/Retna Ltd.: pp. 43, 50 (bottom); Harry Benson: pp. 44–45; Darryl Pitt/Retna Ltd.: pp. 46, 81 (bottom); Andrea Laubach/Retna Ltd.: p. 49; Ken Regan/Columbia Records © 1985 CBS Inc.: p. 50 (top); Care Photo by Nick Blair: p. 52; Larry Busacca/Retna Ltd.: pp. 57, 61 (top); Diamonds and Rust Productions, Inc.: p. 60 (left); David Plastik/Retna Ltd.: p. 61 (bottom); Scott Weiner/Retna Ltd.: pp. 63, 82; Care Photo by Peter Reitz: p. 64; Tom Reusche/Retna Ltd.: p. 74.

Library of Congress Cataloging-in-Publication Data

Berger, Gilda.
USA for Africa.

Includes index.
Summary: Discusses fund-raising concerts and records produced by popular musicians to benefit charities, including projects such as Band Aid, Live Aid, Farm Aid, and others.
1. Rock music—History and criticism—Juvenile literature.   2. Fund raising—Juvenile literature.
3. Benefit performances—Juvenile literature.
4. Africa—Economic conditions—Juvenile literature.
[1. Rock music. 2. Fund raising. 3. Benefit performances] I. Title.
ML3534.B465   1987   784.5′4′00973   86-24718
ISBN 0-531-10299-8

CONTENTS

USA FOR AFRICA

PART

INTRODUCTION

ONE

THE SPIRIT
OF THE
EIGHTIES

"A funny thing happened to the world in 1985," said veteran singer Harry Belafonte. "It cared."

Rock musicians, pop stars, and hordes of their young fans gave a new look to the 1980s. They proved that rock music could do more than entertain or shock and outrage listeners. They showed that rock stars could get people all over the world involved and working to help those in need. In a series of historic events, the leading pop performers and their young fans came together to try to make things better—in Ethiopia, in South Africa, at home—wherever people were hungry or oppressed.

A group of British rock musicians under the name Band Aid started turning things around in late 1984 when they produced a single, "Do They Know It's Christmas?" to raise money for the starving millions in Africa. Early in 1985, over forty-six American stars, calling themselves USA for Africa, cut a record, "We Are the World," with 90 percent of the proceeds also going to African famine relief and the rest to help homeless Americans.

Live Aid in July 1985 was the biggest event in the history of rock. Over 160,000 fans attended twin concerts simultaneously held in Philadelphia and London. Another 1.5 billion watched on TV and heard it on radio in every corner of the globe.

In September 1985, Farm Aid, a rock concert lasting nearly fifteen hours, was given in Illinois, the center of the farm belt. Its purpose was to make the public aware of the farmer's plight, as well as to raise millions of dollars to provide emergency help for struggling American farmers. The next month the album and single, *Sun City*, was released, raising a searing cry against the apartheid system and racial discrimination in South Africa.

And early in 1986, the fervor for caring and compassion reached an even greater height with Hands Across America, the biggest participatory event of all time. Nearly five million men, women, and children (not to mention ten elephants) attempted to form a 4,150-mile (6,677-km) chain across the United States to collect money for America's needy.

To understand how rock music helped bring about the new spirit of the eighties, we have to first look at its history.

Rock 'n' roll began in the early 1950s. It grew out of rhythm and blues, a kind of music that combined country and gospel lyrics with a strong, steady, rhythmic beat.

Many consider Bill Haley the first "star" of rock 'n' roll. His hit tunes, "Shake, Rattle and Roll" and "Rock Around the Clock," were loud, rhythmic, and good for dancing. But Bill Haley could hardly compare to the real king of rock—Elvis Presley. Presley came along in 1954 and made rock 'n' roll *the* music of young people and a symbol of their rebellion.

Presley added a raw sexual energy to the excitement of rhythm and blues. Young people loved to watch him perform "Heartbreak Hotel," "Don't Be Cruel," and "Hound Dog," among many other songs. The fact that Boston religious leaders urged that rock 'n' roll be banned and a Hartford psychiatrist called it a "communicable disease" only led teens to buy more Presley records than before.

Artists such as Pat Boone, Ricky Nelson, Paul Anka, and Frankie Avalon were also on the charts at the time. Their songs—"Teen Queen," "Teen Angel," and "At the Hop"—were far tamer and more restrained than Presley's tunes. Like most songs of the fifties, the lyrics focused on love, loneliness, and the break-up of teenage romances.

Two major streams flowed into the river of rock 'n' roll in the sixties. The first was folk music, represented by such singers as Pete Seeger and by such groups as the Weavers, the Kingston Trio, and Peter, Paul, and Mary. Folk songs were sung on college campuses, at concerts, and at informal song fests called hootenannies. Record sales soared.

The honesty of the lyrics was especially appealing in the mid-sixties, a time of widespread anger and confusion over the war in Vietnam. New performers, especially Bob Dylan, Simon and Garfunkel, and Joan Baez, included social messages in the folk-style songs they sang. In time, such protest songs as "If I Had a Hammer" (Peter, Paul, and Mary) and "Where Have All the Flowers Gone?" (Kingston Trio) gave way to folk rock. Singers such as Dylan, Sonny and Cher, and Buffy Saint-Marie added electric guitar and the advanced harmonies and rhythms of rock 'n' roll to their songs of social concern.

The second big stream of the sixties was best represented by the Beatles. They burst on the scene with an original and exuberant style.

Bill Haley (holding guitar) of Bill Haley and the Comets

Elvis Presley

Pat Boone (left) and Paul Anka

Above: *Sonny and Cher.* Opposite: *Paul Simon
(on left) and Art Garfunkel*

The Beatles. From left to right: *Paul McCartney, John Lennon, Ringo Starr, and George Harrison*

Almost at once, they broke down all barriers between performer and listener, bringing much of the world together with their music.

The Beatles, along with other performers of the sixties, changed the point of rock lyrics. They brought a fresh current of ideas into the mainstream of American life. They also sang of love, but in a new and different way.

The Beatles' songs were sophisticated, poetic, and witty. They poked fun at traditional boy-girl relationships. They criticized social conformity and promoted equality between the sexes. They spoke of peace and freedom, and of an end to war and economic greed. By showing that they were unafraid to deal with the real issues of their time, the Beatles led others to do likewise.

A generation of "flower children" grew up in the sixties, dedicated to some of the highest moral and ethical ideals. But this started to change toward the end of the decade. Protests on behalf of social, racial, and political freedom began to die out. Many young people got involved with drugs. Instead of working to build a better world, they sought to increase their own pleasure and satisfaction. The slogan coined by Timothy Leary, a leader in the drug movement, "Turn on, tune in, drop out," became the rallying cry of many of the young people.

With the Beatles' breakup in 1970, many performers and young people alike drifted toward apathy and isolation. Music lost its special way of binding young people together. Social concerns and good causes now seemed to matter far less than just feeling good. The high-minded vision that had sustained rock for a decade began to fall apart.

The music of the seventies was increasingly characterized by despair and disillusion. It reflected the souring of joyful and trusting feelings. Acid rock, music closely associated with the drug experience, became popular. Records with such suggestive titles as "Good Vibrations" (Beach Boys), "Mother's Little Helper" (Rolling Stones), and "Rainy Day Woman" (Bob Dylan) show the change.

Even so, there were artists—and fans—who kept rock's tradition of social activism alive in the late sixties and seventies. A rock festival held in San Francisco in June 1967 collected about $200,000 for charity. In 1971 Phil Spector produced a concert with George Harrison at Madison Square Garden in New York and raised over $240,000 for the starving in Bangladesh. More than a million dollars of record album profits from the Bangladesh concert were donated to UNICEF. Also in the seventies, the Rolling Stones held a concert in Los Angeles for Nicaraguan earthquake victims and contributed $200,000 to the cause. Lead singer Mick Jagger added another $150,000 of his own money. In 1979 Musicians United for Safe Energy (MUSE), featuring Bruce Springsteen and Jackson Browne, netted over $250,000 at a Madison Square Garden concert to help finance antinuclear groups.

Some rock stars of the 1970s, though, followed the style and sounds of the fifties. Their music became known as pop rock. Pop rock generally combined the main subject of pop songs—sentimental love—with a rock beat. Barry Manilow ranked very high in pop rock with "Tryin' to Get the Feelin'," "Beautiful Music," and "Looks Like We Made It"—solid hits that were innocent, and very appealing.

Another style, known as disco, tried to recapture the excitement of rock in the 1960s. Despite the lonely, self-centered sentiment of the seventies, a time period which writer Tom Wolfe characterized as the "Me Decade," disco's hammering beat created a kind of artificial energy. The film score of *Saturday Night Fever* and singles by Donna Summer were top-of-the-chart disco selections.

The end of the seventies and the start of the eighties saw the emergence of punk rock. This action-packed music strove to stun and overwhelm its listeners. Bizarre dress and disturbing behavior on stage and off was the prevailing style. The musicians seemed to emphasize the more commercial aspects of their music—glitter over substance, excitement for excitement's sake, and an overall "grab the money and run" approach. Critics accused them of having a kind of "bubblegum" mentality. Recently rock singer Little Steven described that period as "ten to fifteen years of being in a coma."

Then, in 1984, rock music began to turn around. It seemed to awaken from a long, deep sleep with a new conscience. "Rock Flexed Its Social and Political Muscles," read a *New York Times* headline in January 1986.

A sense of excitement and commitment to the ideals of the sixties spread through the music community. Bob Geldof, an Irish rock performer who led the group Boomtown Rats, was a prime mover in this turnaround. He said, "It has become fashionable to care again." The benefit records and concerts of the mid-1980s signaled a change in direction away from the self-centered outlook of the seventies. The caring and sharing attitudes of the earlier years were reborn.

Of course, the eighties are not exactly like the sixties. Today's rock is far less stormy and fiery than before. It is more "comfortable and accessible," in the words of Mary Travers from the group Peter, Paul, and Mary. "The big difference between now and the sixties," Bob Dylan said, "is that then it was much more dangerous to do that sort of thing. There was a lot more violence." Don Henley, one of the leading performers at Farm Aid, put it another way. He said that the spirit of the eighties was "a little more

Above: *Bruce Springsteen.*
Below: *Donna Summer*

20

pragmatic." That is to say, the activists of today have a more down-to-earth view of what they can hope to accomplish.

Still, this is a very important time for pop music. The technological marvel of instant worldwide satellite communication is bringing the whole world closer together. Rock music has already shown that it is able to make people think and move forward. It can act as a unifying force rather than a divisive one. Once more rock and youth are leading the way. They are transforming the culture. At the same time they are changing the people of America—and of the world.

PART

ROCK FOR
AFRICA

Above: *death in a dried-up waterhole near Gedaref in the Sudan.* Below: *destitute drought victims camping on a roadside in Wellow Province, Ethiopia*

TWO

THE AGONY
OF AFRICA

Africa is a difficult continent on which to live. The climate can be very harsh. Some areas are extremely hot all year round. Others have either too much or too little rain. The deserts and forests that cover much of the land are fit neither for farming nor cattle grazing. The dangers of drought, disease, and famine are always present and have struck with deadly results many times in recent years. The death rate is higher and the life expectancy is lower there than anywhere else on earth.

For the first half of the twentieth century most of Africa was under European colonial control. During this time there were many improvements in communication, transportation, sanitation, health care, education, commerce, and industry. And the continent was self-sufficient as far as food was concerned. About four of every five Africans, women and men, made their living by farming, growing enough food or raising enough cattle to feed their own families.

But during this same period the black population of Africa endured much pain and humiliation. Completely under the domination of white Europeans, they were deprived of basic freedoms and lacked any opportunities to improve their situation. Racial discrimination was common and political activity was not allowed.

By the end of World War II, in 1945, black Africans were beginning to increasingly demand self-government. The colonial powers made some efforts to raise living standards and give Africans a larger role in government. But in most cases they did too little and acted too late. Starting around 1950, colony after colony, either by violent or peaceful means, won its freedom from foreign domination.

With independence came many changes and some improvements. Over the next thirty years life expectancy rose from 39 to more than 53 years. Infant mortality dropped from 169 to 115 per thousand births. The percentage of children attending primary school rose from 32 to 80 percent and of those attending secondary school from 3 to 22 percent. Roads and dams were built, telephone lines were strung, and the standard of living rose.

But government leaders, often under the guidance of European colonialists, made some disastrous economic decisions. Instead of trying to make their nations agriculturally self-sufficient, they embarked on grandiose industrial and manufacturing schemes similar to ones set up by the more technologically advanced nations. They tried to introduce modern machinery and means of production. But shortages of skilled labor and management, scarcity of spare parts, and other problems doomed these projects to failure.

At the same time there was a growing need for food around the world. There were huge profits to be made in growing food. Investors started buying up African farmland. They transformed African agriculture from small-scale subsistence farming, which had fed the Africans reasonably well for many generations, into large-scale plantation farming of export crops, such as cocoa, cotton, and peanuts. The government kept the price of food artificially low to earn greater profits from overseas sales and to provide cheap food for city dwellers.

As an outcome of these policies, some people grew immensely wealthy. For the small-scale farmers, though, the results were disastrous. They earned far less than it cost them to grow the crops. In an effort to survive, they tried raising crops on land fit only for grazing—and ruined the soil for all uses.

Facing starvation, a great many men, women, and children from the rural farming areas of Africa were forced to leave the land and seek jobs in the already overcrowded cities. Lacking money for proper housing, they built dwellings that became huge shantytowns, collections of miserable little huts made of scrap materials and having no water or electricity.

Also, the bloodshed and violence that accompanied the overthrow of some of the colonial powers continued into the new regimes. Many of the emerging nations modeled their governments on European and American systems. But these systems in general did not work well under the specific conditions of life in Africa. Finally, there was much ethnic and religious strife within some countries and between neighboring countries.

During the mid-1960s, the governments of several African countries were overthrown. Military takeovers by powerful leaders established authoritarian regimes in many of the newly formed nations.

Above and over: *scenes from various reception centers for refugees and feeding stations in drought-stricken Africa. Disease and death are constant companions to the people in these relief camps. The old woman above has her head shaved to control lice.*

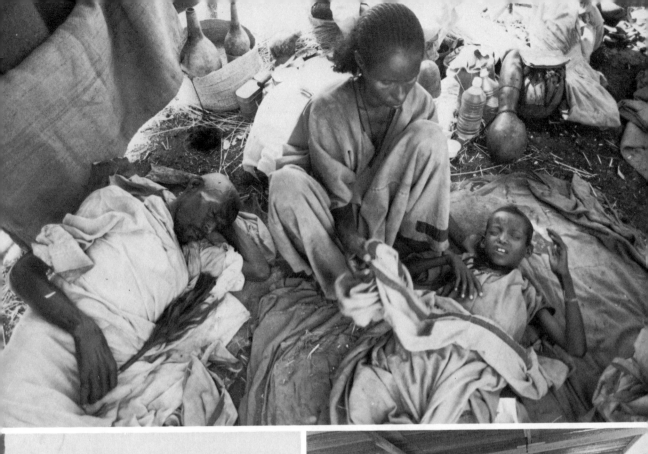

Throughout this entire period, shortages of food kept mounting. The situation was made even worse by an accelerating birth rate, higher than on any other continent. Because each African family had an average of six children, there were at least one million new mouths to feed every month! Africa's economic development just could not keep pace with its rapid population growth. During these years, too, the deserts were spreading, destroying more and more farmland. And entire forests were being cut down and burned in wasteful, inefficient open fires for cooking and heating.

Added to this rapidly deteriorating situation was one of the worst droughts in history. Starting in 1981, the rainfall was far below average for four consecutive years. The year 1984 was the worst of all, with many areas not getting as much as one drop of rain. Although the following year was better, crop production still fell far short of the people's needs.

To make matters worse, there were, and continue to be, fierce civil wars raging in areas of Ethiopia and the Sudan. Also, the drought is the worst in remote regions that are extremely difficult to reach with supplies. And finally, because of war and drought, vast numbers of people have left their villages and their small farms and now depend completely on government relief.

The result? Africa has become the only continent in the world where farmers now produce less food per person than they did twenty years earlier. The standard of living, which was never very high, is falling. Hundreds of thousands of Africans have already died of starvation. The famine produced thousands of orphans and hundreds of thousands of refugees. The United Nations estimates that about twenty million more are in desperate need of food, medical supplies, health care, and water.

Until 1984, most of the world knew little of the horrible pain and suffering raging in Africa. But in October of that year British television showed a nightmarish documentary that pictured hordes of thin, withered, starving Ethiopians living in desolate camps. The sight of those suffering people pricked the consciences of many viewers. But none acted more quickly and with better results than Bob Geldof, lead singer of the Irish rock group, the Boomtown Rats. Geldof, more than anyone else, roused the conscience of the world to save the helpless victims from hunger and starvation.

Bob Geldof

THREE

BAND AID: THE BRITISH EFFORT

"I often wonder," Irish rock star Bob Geldof confessed, "what would have happened had I not been in that night."

The night he was referring to was in October 1984. British television was airing a horrifying report on the starving millions in drought-stricken east Africa, particularly Ethiopia.

"The thing I remember most," Geldof recalled, "was the picture of the wall. There were about ten thousand people there, starving people, and there was this woman—who I subsequently met—who had to pick three hundred people that she could feed. The three hundred were led behind a stone wall, and each was given a can of butter oil, because that's all there was to eat.

"And the ones who hadn't been picked stood up behind the waist-high wall and looked at them, without any rancor or envy, but with intense dignity. That waist-high wall was the difference between life and death. And I remember seeing one child just put her head against the wall, the flies buzzing around her eyes. That's what made me do it. That one image is what made me do the whole thing."

"The whole thing" was an all-out effort to raise funds to bring much-needed food and supplies to the African victims. Geldof decided to write and record a song and use all of the proceeds for famine relief in Africa. At the time Geldof was working with the Boomtown Rats on a song entitled "It's My World." During a twenty-minute taxi ride to the recording studio he rewrote the lyrics. The words "feed the world" now became the urgent

Above: *the group "Band Aid."*
Opposite: *Duran Duran*

This "hunger walk" shows a starving refugee and her child heading toward a feeding center in the Eastern Sudan.

message of the song. Later he changed the title to "Do They Know It's Christmas?" A good friend of Bob's, Midge Ure of the rock group Ultravox, helped him finish the song.

Geldof asked a number of his rock friends to join his group in recording the song. A string of stars immediately responded to his call. Boy George said he would fly back to London from New York for the recording session. Duran Duran would return from West Germany; U2 said they would come over from Ireland. Altogether thirty-eight top British rockers agreed to pitch in to cut the record. In this stellar lineup of British rock stars were Phil Collins, Paul Young, Wham!, and Culture Club. Kool and the Gang, from America, also joined in. In the words of Sting, then of The Police, the group wanted "to raise enough money to mean something."

The group took the name "Band Aid" partly in fun. They were indeed a *band* coming to the *aid* of the Africans. But the help they were offering could only make a tiny difference in the face of such enormous need. As Geldof said, "There's no use putting a band-aid on a wound that requires twenty stitches."

The record "Do They Know It's Christmas?" was cut on November 25, 1984. It became an instant hit. Disc jockeys played it constantly on the radio; it was featured in dozens of newspaper and magazine articles. In England it was the hit single of 1984, selling three and one-half million copies. Another two and one-half million were sold in America, bringing the total proceeds to about $11 million.

Meanwhile, Geldof took a trip to Ethiopia and the Sudan. His purpose was to see for himself how the money they had raised could best be used. He visited the camps and the villages to try to understand the problem. He met with government officials. And he spoke with representatives of the big international relief agencies.

He ultimately decided that the Band Aid money should be used to buy food and supplies and deliver them directly to the people in need. He set up the Band Aid Trust, with prominent figures from the world of business and government to oversee its operation. The trust became the chief means for delivering the aid to Africa.

Geldof's efforts succeeded far beyond his wildest dreams. If Band Aid had only raised millions for African relief, that would have been achievement enough. But it did much, much more. As Harry Belafonte said, "Band Aid . . . lit a fuse of compassion that burned around the world."

Lionel Richie (left) and Harry Belafonte

FOUR

USA FOR AFRICA: THE AMERICAN EFFORT

Harry Belafonte is known to millions as an extremely talented singer and actor. But even his most devoted fans may not know of his far-ranging humanitarian work—in the Peace Corps, in the civil rights movement, and through the contributions of the Belafonte Foundation to various worthwhile projects.

Late in 1984 Belafonte was greatly troubled by news of the devastating famine in Ethiopia. He was aware, too, of the sensational success of British performer Bob Geldof and Band Aid in raising funds for Africa.

Around Christmas 1984 Belafonte called Ken Kragen, the manager of such stars as Lionel Richie and Kenny Rogers, all of whom were known as supporters of worthy causes. Belafonte proposed an all-star concert of black American performers in New York City's Madison Square Garden.

Kragen argued against the concert idea. It was "too complicated," he said. But he was all for cutting a record. "Bob Geldof had found the key," said Kragen. They agreed that this record should include America's top rock stars, both black *and* white. And they decided to call it "USA for Africa," short for United Support of Artists for Africa.

The very next day, Kragen got the ball rolling by speaking to Lionel Richie about writing the song. Richie said yes at once. Kragen also asked Quincy Jones, a top record producer and Grammy Award winner, to be music director. Since Quincy had worked with Michael Jackson on Jackson's last two albums, Quincy talked Jackson into co-writing the song with Richie.

Richie and Jackson had some trouble getting started, but gradually, the song began to take shape. Some random bits of melody that Lionel had taped inspired Michael to start writing. By the end of just one day he had the melody line for the whole song! A date was set to make a demo tape—even though the lyrics were still not written. In two-and-a-half hours of hard work, the day before the taping, they finished the words.

Richie and Jackson, with producer Jones, got together to tape a rough version of "We Are the World." They ordered fifty copies to help them recruit other stars. The rough recording was pretty good by itself. When Bob Dylan heard it, he asked Kragen, "Well—what do you want *me* to do?"

Dylan, of course, soon got the idea and signed up. So did over forty of the biggest names in American rock music. But this had to be a group effort. Quincy Jones sent out the message: "Check your egos at the door."

One big question still remained: How could all these incredibly busy artists be brought together in one place at one time? Even though he did not know it at the time, TV producer and host Dick Clark had the perfect solution. On January 28, 1985, his show, the *American Music Awards*, was being telecast from Los Angeles. Many of the performers who would be on the "We Are the World" recording were planning to be there.

As soon as Kragen heard this, he arranged for the free use of the Los Angeles A & M Recording Studios for the late evening, after the TV show. A & M was his first choice because it had only one small entrance. The single door could easily be secured from the multitude of uninvited fans who were sure to show up as soon as word of the recording session got out.

As soon as the time, place, and talent were set, Quincy Jones and vocal arranger Tom Bahler began the staggering task of assigning the vocal parts. As Jones put it, "It's like putting a watermelon in a Coke bottle." At the same time, Ken Kragen and his crew started working out the details of transportation, food, security, press coverage, and so on.

By eight o'clock on January 28 the technical crew was almost done setting up its equipment for the big event. Quincy Jones and James Ingram were the first to arrive, followed by Michael Jackson at nine. Jones and Jackson plunged right in, putting the final touches on the background harmonies. The three Pointer Sisters came next, followed by Bruce Springsteen, who flew in especially for the recording and drove himself to the studio. Because they didn't want to disturb Jones and Jackson, the Pointer Sisters and Springsteen went to the control room. The room had only three chairs, so June Pointer offered to share her chair with Bruce. "That was the end," she later said.

Michael Jackson

More musical superstars were taking part in USA for Africa than for any other single event in the history of rock music. By 10:30 the parking lot was filled to overflowing with limousines and sleek sports cars. The performers' friends (each star was allowed to invite five guests) gathered in a lounge to watch the proceedings on a big TV screen. A camera crew was set up in the studio to film the event.

As the stars kept gathering, they squeezed themselves into the control room. The room became so crowded that someone humorously called it the first example of "star-lock."

"Let's move into the studio, *please*," Quincy Jones shouted out over the chatter. The artists drifted slowly into the large room. They looked at the little name strips that were already in place on the risers that lined one side of the studio. All took their assigned places, without grumbling. Some of the biggest names ended up in the back rows, instead of front and center as usual.

Ken Kragen set the right tone at the outset. "What's going to come from this night is a lot more than money," he said. "It's a commitment and the ability to move people. To show the way. To stay on the case. You create a power where we can go forward and inspire people. What we're doing is far more significant than just a song, or raising money. We're making a statement."

Then, eager to get started, Quincy Jones got up on the podium in front of the star-studded chorus. "OK, let's start chopping wood."

With the downbeat, the forty-three voices of this million-dollar chorus rose over the prerecorded backup track. Take followed take as Jones, with the help of Richie and Jackson, worked to get it technically and musically perfect.

About midnight, Quincy Jones called a break. A few of the performers walked into the lounge to visit with their guests, who included Jane Fonda, Steve Martin, Brooke Shields, and Kareem Abdul-Jabbar.

A very special spirit filled the studio. The forty individual stars felt like part of one big, happy family. Bette Midler and Paul Simon, for example, who had been feuding, called a truce. "We've been small-mouthing each other for years," explained Bette, "but it was such a warm occasion, we sort of buried the hatchet."

Inspired by Diana Ross, almost everyone went around collecting autographs on their song sheets. Compliments flowed—"I love your song," "I've been wanting to meet you," "Man, you've got a great set of pipes," "I have always been a fan of yours," and so on. Bob Dylan, who played harmonica on a 1961 Harry Belafonte recording, wrote on Belafonte's music sheet, "Thanks for giving me my start."

The emotions grew stronger. Many of the singers gathered around Ray Charles, who was jamming on the studio piano. Bette Midler perhaps put

Above: *The Pointer Sisters.*
Over: *A group shot of the
"We Are the World" singers*

Above: *Diana Ross.* Opposite: *Bette Midler*

it best: "It was heartbreaking, just beautiful. There wasn't a dry eye in the house."

There was a lavish buffet—all donated—of imported cheeses, huge bowls of caviar, and the finest pastries. Bob Geldof, who had just seen Africans dying of starvation before his eyes, was struck by the contrast between the bounty on this table and the critical shortages of food abroad.

Springsteen was also very moved by what was happening in that room. A long-time fighter in the battle against hunger, he had donated large sums to food banks, shelters for the homeless, and other projects in almost every town he visited during his successful 1985 American tour. Speaking of his sadness at the world's indifference to famine, he said, "There's all this senseless suffering in the world. Either you're tearing something down or building something up. I want to be part of that building process. Holding back the flood a little bit."

By one A.M. everyone was back on the risers. The taping of the chorus took two more hours to complete. While everyone freshened up, the photographers were called in to take pictures for the album cover and poster.

A very big job—the duets and solos—still had to be done. Stevie Wonder and Lionel Richie, Kenny Rogers and Paul Simon, Michael Jackson and Diana Ross, Cyndi Lauper and Huey Lewis, Willie Nelson and Dionne Warwick, Tina Turner and Billy Joel, and others—all took their turn in pairs. The excitement was contagious. "It was only four words," Billy Joel later said, "but as far as I'm concerned, I did a duet with Tina Turner."

The soloists were set to record when two Ethiopian girls, guests of Stevie Wonder, walked into the room. What followed was called by James Ingram "the most magical point of the night." Stevie Wonder introduced the two visitors to the group.

"Thank you on behalf of everyone from our country," one girl said shyly, her lips trembling. First in Amharic, their language, and then in English, each girl struggled to find the words to express her gratitude. The artists were deeply affected. No one spoke.

"It was just so touching, that at that moment I didn't see one superstar in the room," said Ingram. "I saw tears in a lot of people's eyes."

There was absolute silence in the room after the girls left. Quincy Jones finally broke into the quiet. "It's time to sing," he said softly.

For nearly three more hours, the various soloists did many takes of their few lines. It was hard work, but everyone was giving it his or her very best. The fancy food was long-since gone. Brenda Richie sent out for a stack of hamburgers.

At one point an engineer stopped the recording. A rattling noise, a sort of clanking and tinkling, had crept into the equipment. Frantically, the work-

Cyndi Lauper

ers tested the mikes, cables, and electronic equipment to see what was causing the racket. They found nothing.

Finally, someone discovered the problem. Billy Joel later described the scene: "After four takes they realized that the clanking noise was Cyndi's [Lauper] jewelry." The engineer said to her, "Look, I love your jewelry, but let's face it. On this microphone, it sounds like a train wreck." Cyndi slipped off her trademark jewelry to some good-natured kidding.

The soloists plugged away at their lines through the wee hours of the morning. Lionel Richie, Stevie Wonder, Paul Simon, Kenny Rogers, James Ingram, Tina Turner, Billy Joel, Diana Ross, Dionne Warwick, and the others stepped up to the mikes, one after the other. Some of the most experienced performers had trouble deciding how to deliver their lines. During one unforgettable moment, Stevie Wonder coached Bob Dylan on how to sound more like Bob Dylan!

Those who finished their parts hugged Quincy and each other and drifted out to the waiting limousines. By 8 A.M. it was all over. Quincy Jones called out the magical words, "That's a take!" The most memorable, all-night recording session in music history had come to an end.

The single "We Are the World" was shipped to the record stores on March 7, 1985. It sold an astounding million-plus copies the first week alone! In a few weeks it was the best-selling single in America and went on to become one of the fastest-selling singles of all time. In a unique symbolic gesture, eight thousand radio stations all around the world played "We Are the World" simultaneously on Good Friday, April 5, 1985, at exactly 10:50 A.M., Eastern Daylight Time. The song won a Grammy Award as the best song of 1985.

The disk had sold nearly ten million copies by the beginning of 1986. To this incredible figure must be added the sales of the *We Are the World* album, which includes other songs by artists on the record, and the one-hour video that was shot during the recording session. Further income came from the sale of T-shirts, sweat shirts, posters, and other related merchandise. The total proceeds were estimated at over $44 million!

Of the total sum, about $8 million went directly for emergency aid in Ethiopia, the Sudan, and other nations of Africa. Close to $7 million was

Above: *Bob Dylan.* Below (left to right): *Quincy Jones, Dionne Warwick, Michael Jackson, Stevie Wonder, and Lionel Richie accept the Grammy Award for "We Are the World."*

spent on the means to deliver the aid—trucks, ships, fuel, spare parts, and so on. Most of the remaining money is being used for long-term projects, such as roads, dams, dikes, irrigation projects, and education. About 10 percent is being used to help the needy in the United States. Once more, Harry Belafonte summed it up best: "We are all brothers. We are responsible for one another. Truly, we are the world."

*Donations of food and grain
help relieve the starvation in
famine-ridden areas of Africa.*

FIVE

LIVE AID:
A WORLDWIDE
EFFORT

Band Aid and USA for Africa inspired a worldwide outpouring of food, money, sympathy, and publicity for Africa's victims. In Melbourne, Australia, over one hundred performers raised about $2 million in a concert called EAT, standing for East Africa Tragedy. Dozens of stars in Toronto, Canada, recorded a single, "Tears Are Not Enough," for Ethiopian famine relief. American heavy-metal performers put on Hear 'n' Aid. And musicians in at least twenty other countries contributed their talent to help the cause. Yet lots more still had to be done to eliminate the staggering problems of African poverty, illness, and starvation.

Nobody knew more about hunger in Ethiopia, the Sudan, Chad, Mozambique, and other parts of Africa than Bob Geldof. He had traveled to the continent and visited the refugee camps and spoken to relief workers. He saw tens of thousands of living skeletons that reminded him of Nazi concentration camps. He saw sick children with swollen bellies and vacant eyes. He saw rusting trucks and farm machines that had lain idle for months waiting for scarce diesel fuel.

Geldof had succeeded beyond his greatest dreams with Band Aid. But he knew that millions of dollars more were needed. At the "We Are the World" recording session he proposed an even more stupendous rock event. Two concerts would be given at the same time—one in England, one in America. They would be linked up by satellite and shown on TV in countries throughout the world. Dozens of top rock stars from both sides of the Atlantic would perform live before many thousands of fans. And a worldwide TV audience of over one billion would watch and be encouraged to contribute money to help the needy in Africa.

Harvey Goldsmith is England's biggest promoter of rock concerts. With Geldof, they set a date—July 13, 1985. This left very little time in which to pull together the thousands of separate strands needed for an event of this scope. Geldof and Goldsmith worked the English end—getting Wembley Stadium in London as the site, lining up the performers, arranging for the light and sound equipment, and covering all the other necessary details.

On the American side, Bill Graham, the veteran rock concert producer, took charge. He agreed to rent Philadelphia's John F. Kennedy Stadium and to oversee the artistic aspects. Michael C. Mitchell, head of Worldwide Sports and Entertainment, handled all the business and financial matters. He also set up the TV network that would link London and Philadelphia and beam the concert to every corner of the world.

On June 10, 1985, at news conferences in London and Philadelphia, Geldof announced Live Aid to the world. He described it as a "global jukebox."

As July 13 neared, Bill Graham realized that nearly one hundred of the biggest rock acts of all time had offered to appear in Philadelphia. But there just wasn't enough time to fit them all in. He had the tough job of cutting the list down to just thirty-nine acts.

A few big names were missing. Bruce Springsteen didn't come because he had promised his band a vacation, and he didn't want to go back on his word. Lionel Richie's band wasn't together, and he didn't want to appear without them (though he did sing in the final combined number). Billy Joel also refused because he did not want to appear as a solo performer without a band. And Huey Lewis and the News backed out because they were afraid that the money raised would not actually reach the famine victims.

Two concerts and a telethon like Live Aid would normally cost about $20 million to produce. The Philadelphia concert alone required 10 million watts of electricity, 5,000 lights, and over 150 miles (245 km) of electric cable, plus the use of sixteen satellites in space for the global telecast. Remarkably enough, Live Aid only cost about $4 million. This is because everyone pitched in. The performers all appeared without fee, the stadiums charged reduced rents, and the backup staff and suppliers provided the goods and services at little or no cost.

Bob Geldof helps promote products associated with Live Aid, to increase revenues for his life-saving efforts.

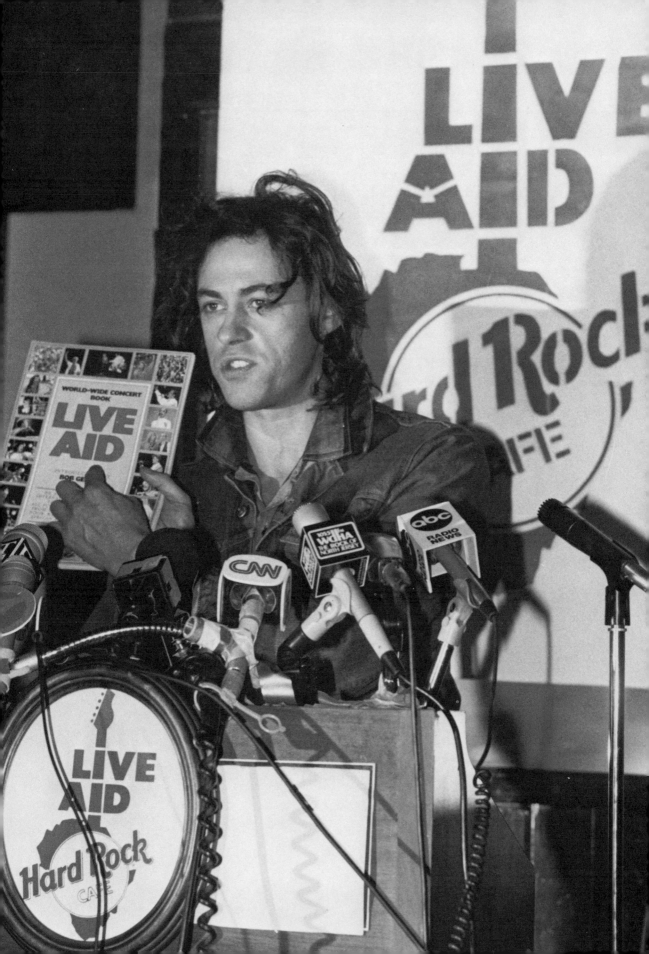

Live Aid at Wembley Stadium in London

The mammoth concert began in Wembley Stadium, London, at noon (7 A.M. in Philadelphia). It was opened by Prince Charles and Princess Diana.

Jack Nicholson opened the American show at 9 A.M. He introduced Joan Baez, who invoked the spirit of the sixties. She said, "We will reach deep into our hearts and our souls and say that we will move a little from the comfort of our lives to understand their hurt."

From early morning until 11 o'clock that night, superstar followed superstar in two amazing parades of pop music talent. While stars performed in London, the crowd in Philadelphia watched them on the giant TV screen in JFK Stadium. When musicians were on stage in Philadelphia, London viewed them on the Wembley Stadium TV monitor. Meanwhile, over a billion more, in some 130 countries of the world, listened on radios and kept their TVs tuned to the fabulous show.

The lineup of stars was truly incredible. Among the *most* spectacular and unforgettable moments were:

Tina Turner and Mick Jagger, two of the legendary figures of rock, burning up the stage with a sizzling rendition of "State of Shock."

Robert Plant and Jimmy Page of Led Zeppelin coming together for a reunion and doing their hit song, "Stairway to Heaven."

A bearded Elvis Costello emotionally singing the great Beatles' number, "All You Need Is Love," with acoustic guitar.

Phil Collins appearing in London, hopping on the supersonic Concorde jet to America, and later appearing in Philadelphia.

90,000 voices chanting, "Teddy! Teddy! Teddy!" as the tearful, wheelchair-bound Teddy Pendergrass made his first stage appearance since his near-fatal auto accident.

Patti LaBelle shaking and wringing wet after singing "Over the Rainbow."

David Bowie dashing off to his dressing room, where he broke down and cried from the emotional strain of the occasion.

Paul McCartney making his first live concert appearance in seven years with the immortal Beatle tune, "Let It Be."

Bob Dylan doing his classic, "Blowin' in the Wind," backed by Keith Richards and Ron Wood of the Rolling Stones.

The London show ending with the entire cast singing the song that had started it all, "Do They Know It's Christmas?"

Everyone sang "We Are the World" to close in Philadelphia.

Above left: *Joan Baez opened the singing at JFK Stadium in Philadelphia.* Above right: *Mick Jagger and Tina Turner.*
Opposite: *Phil Collins (top) and Paul McCartney*

Many consider Live Aid the greatest day in the history of rock. It showed the world that rock artists were willing to take an active part in solving some of the world's more serious problems. When Bob Geldof first announced Live Aid in June, he forecast it would raise about $10 million for Africa's starving. By early 1986, though, Live Aid had actually raised over $80 million!

Geldof once said, "Music can't change the world." But he proved himself wrong. He had used music to change the world and touch people's lives. At a press conference held after Band Aid, Geldof spoke of at least two lives that were changed. He described what he had observed from an airplane flying over the dry, parched land of eastern Africa.

"At one point," he said, "I saw a woman with two children in the middle of this vast desert. She must have walked, at that point, seventy-five miles, just heading in the direction where she heard there was food. She looked up at the plane. She was heading one way and the plane was heading the other, and she turned and headed in the direction of the plane, followed the plane, because she knew she'd *eventually* get to food and water."

More than half of the monies that came in were contributed by TV viewers in countries around the world. People who were watching were moved by appeals from such world figures as Prime Minister Gandhi of India, Coretta King, widow of the great civil rights leader Martin Luther King, Jr., Nobel Peace Prize winner Bishop Desmond Tutu of South Africa, Nobel Prize-winning scientist Linus Pauling, former soccer great Pele, and Oscar-winning actress Sally Field.

Another $10 million came from the sale of TV rights. The viewers who watched Live Aid set a new record in television history. Live Aid became the most widely seen television broadcast since Neil Armstrong walked on the moon.

Close to $6 million was raised by ticket sales alone. Ninety thousand mostly young people in Philadelphia paid $35 or $50 each to attend the concert; 72,000 fans in London each spent $31. Corporate sponsors added at least another $3 million, and the merchandising of various Live Aid products brought in about $750,000.

Geldof quickly carried out the promise he had made to the young fans who supported Live Aid. He chartered five oceangoing freighters through the Band Aid Trust to carry huge shipments of wheat, powdered milk, clothes, and medicines to Africa. In cooperation with the United Nations and the U.S. government he assembled a fleet of 154 heavy-duty trucks to haul the supplies from the docks to the areas with the greatest need.

By the beginning of 1986, the Band Aid Trust had spent $34 million— faster, more effectively, and more efficiently than anyone would have dreamed possible. The money went to seven African nations—Ethiopia, Mozambique, Chad, Burkina Faso, Niger, Mali, and Sudan. About 60 percent of

The finale at JFK Stadium in Philadelphia

the Live Aid money was earmarked for long-term projects, 20 percent for emergency relief, and 20 percent for transportation.

The world took note of Geldof's accomplishments when officials of three countries—England, Ireland, and Norway—nominated him for the Nobel Peace Prize. A somber Geldof explained the reason behind his actions: "We actually need that crowd that's dying over there as much as they need us. Not for our souls. We need people in Africa for loads of reasons. Because they are worthwhile people, because they can give us beauty and joy that far outweighs any money we could give to help keep them alive. Every death diminishes us." Yet when a TV reporter asked about the Nobel nomination, Geldof tossed it off by saying, "I'm going to go home and sleep." Later he was honored by the United Nations and given its 1985 Special Achievement Award for his work on Live Aid.

Band Aid and Live Aid drained Bob Geldof of strength and money. But the concerts energized and inspired many others. For the first time in a long while, there was hope that one day the lands of Ethiopia and the Sudan might be turned back to the farmers to feed their people. The African poor now had a chance to improve their lot.

A U.S. Senate report said that seven million people had been spared starvation in Ethiopia by "a remarkable success story of international relief." Although about a million of Ethiopia's forty-three million people died in the famine, "the American people can know that their assistance not only got through to the people in need, but that it made a difference between life and death for millions."

Rock music had helped turn people away from despair and toward a concern for others. It had shown the world the power of young people. Through Band Aid, USA for Africa, and Live Aid the future was a little brighter than before.

Above: *village women plant seedlings of Acacia abida trees. These fast-growing trees provide natural windbreaks to protect young crops.* Below: *in this emergency aid program, workers are rebuilding many miles of dikes along the Logona River in Chad.*

PART

THE BEAT
GOES ON

SIX

FARM AID: RELIEF AT HOME

A comment mumbled by Bob Dylan at the end of the Live Aid concert in Philadelphia sparked the next big charity-rock event. Dylan suggested that it would be great if some of the money being raised could go to help the American farmers.

"I didn't think anybody heard me, because I couldn't even hear myself say it," Dylan said. "But it occurred to me at that moment that a lot of money was being raised for people to be self-sufficient. And it came to me that people in this country need to be self-sufficient. I thought it was relevant."

An estimated half-million farmers did, in fact, need relief. Many were in danger of losing their farms. Every day about 250 more farmers, almost all on small, family-operated farms, were going out of business. Some were so deeply in debt, and the value of their land and equipment had dropped so low, that they were just walking away from their farms and leaving everything behind. Others, trying to salvage what they could, were selling out at prices as low as 18 cents on the dollar.

Farmers have always taken on more risks than people in other businesses. An entire crop or herd of cattle can be wiped out by frost, drought, or flood. A sudden dip in the price for farm products may mean financial disaster. Traditionally, farmers have been heavy borrowers from banks. They borrow money during the year and pay it back after the harvest. Farmers also depend on the government for help. Some government agencies guarantee the farmers' loans. Others control farm production by offering farmers subsidies or by paying them *not* to grow crops.

Back in the 1970s farmers enjoyed a period of prosperity. Demand for farm products at home and abroad was high. Government subsidies kept prices up. The value of land was rising every year. In those days it made sense to borrow money to buy more land, equipment, and livestock, and to take advantage of the strong agricultural economy.

Then the recession of 1981–82 hit. Farm income fell. Many farmers were weighed down by huge debts and more land and cattle than they needed or could use. Many farmers could not pay their bills and lost their farms.

Over the following years the situation continued to worsen. Part of the blame could be put on the weather. A devastating series of floods, droughts, and early frosts destroyed crops and killed livestock in various areas around the country. Changes in government policies and a general weakness in national and international economies led to lower prices for farm products at home and fewer sales overseas. The high interest rates of the time, added to other rising costs, also hurt the farmers.

As a result, more and more farmers could not pay off their debts. The banks that lent them the money were foreclosing, taking over the farms and selling them off at auction. Many thousands desperately sought ways to hold off the bill collectors until they could get back on their feet. They organized marches and demonstrations, asking for government help in saving their farms.

Willie Nelson, a leading country singer but formerly a farmer, heard Dylan's remarks at Live Aid. He knew firsthand of the American farmers' overwhelming problems. So he decided to put on a blockbuster show that would let the American public know of the tough times the farmers were having. Along the way, he hoped to raise money to help those with the most desperate needs.

Nelson chose a date—September 22, 1985. And he chose a name—Farm Aid. All that remained was to pull together the concert in less than six weeks!

With the help of rock singers John Cougar Mellencamp and Neil Young, Nelson started lining up the talent for what was called a "spirited celebration of American music." Illinois Governor James R. Thompson offered the use of Memorial Stadium at the University of Illinois in Champaign, Illinois. Nelson arranged for radio and television coverage. Special banks of telephones were put in place to receive the thousands of contributions that were expected.

The show started at a quarter to ten in the morning, despite a drenching rain that continued for the first three hours. None of the performers seemed to mind the nasty weather. Nor did the weather dampen the enthusiasm

*Farmers march in Iowa for a moratorium
on farm foreclosures.*

Above: *tractors parked on the mall near the U.S. Capitol in Washington, D.C., are an attempt by farmers to make the nation more aware of their plight. Opposite: Willie Nelson (top) and Billy Joel*

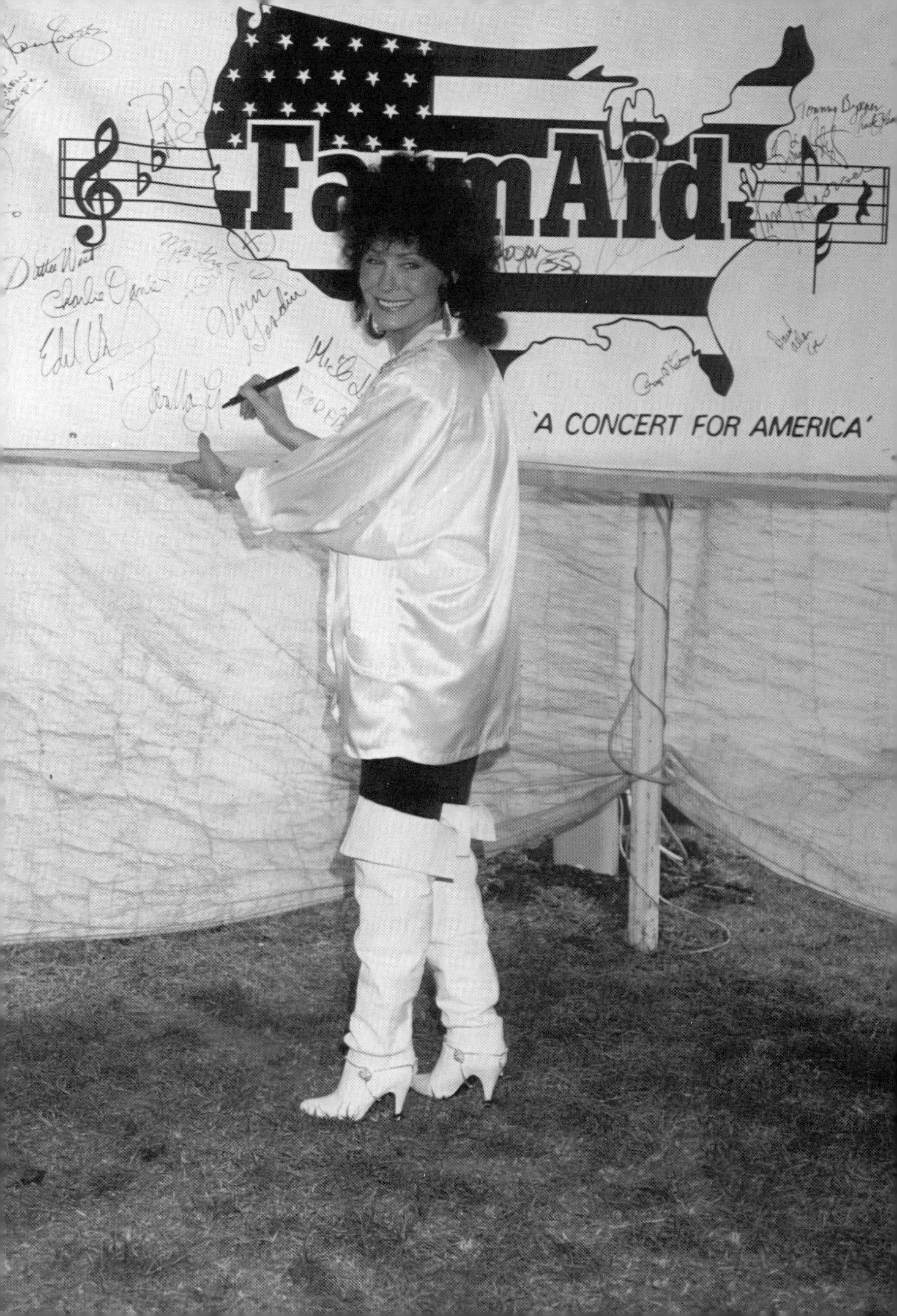
'A CONCERT FOR AMERICA'

Above: *Kenny Rogers.* Opposite: *Loretta Lynn*

of the audience of young fans. "People are listening to what musicians have to say," explained Willie Nelson.

This was a very special concert. It represented a cross section of American pop music. Included were country and western singers, banjo and guitar pickers, rock groups ranging from heavy metal to Los Angeles punk, folk singers, blues singers, and rap groups.

Among the fifty-five headliners who appeared were Alabama, the Beach Boys, Johnny Cash, Bob Dylan, John Fogerty, Arlo Guthrie, Merle Haggard, Billy Joel, B. B. King, Loretta Lynn, Kenny Rogers, and X, along with the organizers, Nelson, Mellencamp, and Young. Sissy Spacek, Debra Winger, and Jessica Lange were the MCs.

Nearly fifteen hours after it began, Nelson closed out the music part of the concert with his quiet, sensitive rendition of "Amazing Grace." As the soft, mournful strains of the song drifted through the huge stadium, everyone remembered why they were there. The evening then ended with a rousing half-hour display of fireworks.

About 78,000 fans paid nearly $1.4 million for tickets. Pledges of contributions collected during the show added another $2 million. Within a few days the total proceeds was close to $10 million. But as Nelson pointed out, the important thing was not the money so much as making people aware of the problem.

Once again, musicians in the pop music world had brought people to the collection box. Breaking down walls between different kinds of music and different parts of the country, they had raised money expressly for poor American farmers. And contributions are still coming in. The performers have vowed not to let the people of America forget the farmers in this, their time of greatest need.

SEVEN

SUN CITY: PROTESTING APARTHEID

Band Aid, USA for Africa, Live Aid, and Farm Aid were calls for charity. But the record "Sun City" was a call for action—for the establishment of racial equality.

The song was written by Little Steven (Steven Van Zandt), who co-produced the record with Arthur Baker. It was released in October 1985. The name refers to a sports and entertainment complex in the so-called black homeland of Bophuthatswana in South Africa, where performers play to mostly white audiences.

"Sun City" is a bold, powerful outcry against apartheid, the official policy of segregation adopted by the white government of South Africa in 1948, which is still in effect today.

The 33 million people of South Africa are divided into four basic groups. By far the largest segment is the blacks, numbering close to 24 million. South African blacks outnumber whites five to one. Although many blacks belong to such ethnic groups as the Zulus, Basutos, Xhosas, and Pondos, they object to the government policy of segregating them according to "tribe."

The nearly 5 million whites are 60 percent Afrikaners and 40 percent Anglos. Afrikaners are the ruling faction of the country. They speak Afrikaans and have deep roots in South Africa. They are the chief supporters of apartheid. In fact, apartheid is an Afrikaans word meaning "apartness" or "separateness." The Anglos, on the other hand, are relative newcomers, speak English, and are eligible for British passports.

The two smaller groups are the 3 million Coloreds, who are of mixed white and black blood, and the 1 million Asians, who are mostly Indians.

According to the laws of apartheid, the blacks can only live in certain designated areas. Over half live in homelands that take up about 13 percent of the land. The rest live in segregated townships that surround the nation's cities.

The blacks are denied many of the rights and privileges enjoyed by other residents of South Africa. Although many blacks work in the cities, none are allowed to live there. The blacks cannot vote in the national elections but can elect the officials of their homelands. They cannot meet in large gatherings, except for sporting events or church services.

By the mid-1980s, black anger over apartheid had boiled over into a true crisis situation. The protest movement escalated in intensity, with violent street demonstrations, boycotts of white businesses, and bitter confrontations with the authorities. The government's response was to become even more restrictive and more brutal in its treatment of the blacks. Beatings, mass arrests, and killings became increasingly commonplace. The voices of moderation on both sides were hooted down as blacks and whites turned to guns and violence to solve their problems.

The police dealt with demonstrators of all ages in a harsh and ruthless manner. In 1985 alone, 201 children were killed by the police. Nineteen of them were under the age of ten. More than 2,000 children were arrested and detained under South Africa's security laws. Two girls, fourteen and sixteen, for example, were held in solitary confinement for seventy-seven days! As in many other cases, the police did not even inform their parents.

In "Sun City" Little Steven took a strong stand on apartheid and hoped to raise money for the struggle against this cruel institution. The lyrics don't mince words: "People are dying and giving up hope." "This quiet diplomacy ain't nothing but a joke." And, perhaps strongest of all, "We're stabbing our brothers and sisters in the back." A far cry indeed from the typically nonpolitical songs of the seventies!

Jazz pianist Herbie Hancock once commented, "Message songs get a little boring. You begin to sound like missionaries." Little Steven made sure that "Sun City" would not be boring. He set the stinging, hard-hitting words over a forceful beat that is great for dancing. To add even more zing, Little Steven got fifty-three top artists, with an exciting mix of styles, to sing or play on the record: Bruce Springsteen and Daryl Hall for mainstream American rock; Ringo Starr and Peter Townsend for English rock; Peter Gabriel for progressive rock; Miles Davis, Herbie Hancock, and Ron Carter for jazz; Jackson Browne and Bonnie Raitt for folk; Ruben Blades

"Miami" Steve Van Zandt

*Violence over apartheid erupts
in Kwa Thema, South Africa*

Above: *Daryl Hall (left) and John Oates.*
Below: *Jimmy Cliff*

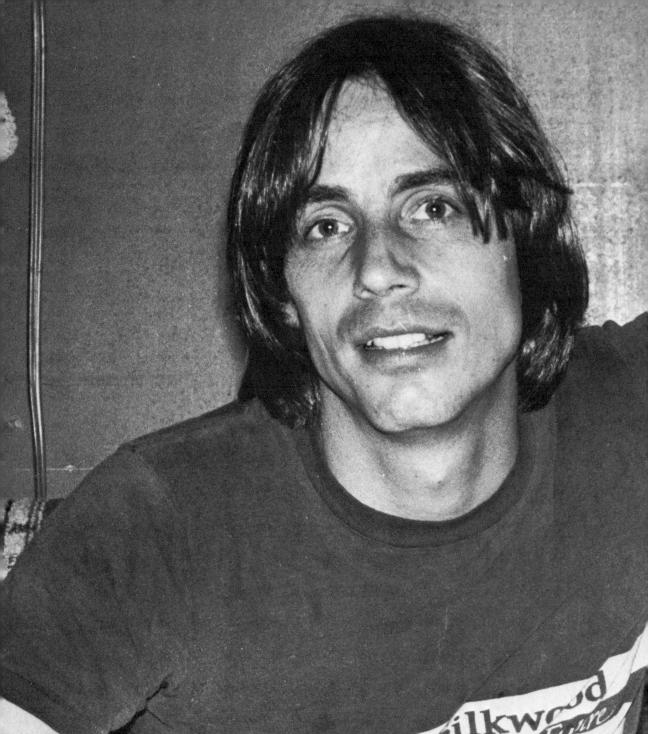

for Latin; Jimmy Cliff for reggae; Ray Barretto for Salsa; Grandmaster Melle Mel for rapping; and a South African group, the Malopoets, among many others.

As with the earlier records and concerts, the all-star cast of "Sun City" worked without fee; many others donated the necessary technical and support equipment and supplies. All of the money raised through the sale of the album goes to the nonprofit Africa Fund and is used to advance the struggle against apartheid.

For a long while people felt that the protest against apartheid was brave but useless. The white regime was so strong that nothing seemed to change, no matter how many lives were lost. But now most agree that significant change has taken place and a point of no return may have been reached. "Sun City" is one symbol of this change. It is a small step in the long journey toward racial equality in South Africa. And it is further evidence that America's rock artists and young people are concerned about the struggle for freedom and justice at home *and* abroad.

On April 18, 1986, the South African government stopped enforcing the pass laws. These hated laws controlled where black people could live and work. For blacks, the pass laws represented perhaps the worst aspect of apartheid. This is definitely a step in the right direction. But most black South Africans still feel they have a long way to go toward a democratic system, free of oppression and fear.

Jackson Browne

EIGHT

HANDS ACROSS AMERICA

Poverty and hunger are problems that exist within the United States as well as abroad. Just now there is much suffering in the communities of America. According to a recent report, up to 20 million Americans, including the unemployed, the working poor, and struggling farmers, are hungry at some time during each month. The most visible part of this poverty group are the homeless—those who have no place to live, except in streets, cars, abandoned buildings, and public shelters. An estimated 2 million people are homeless in America.

In the past most of the homeless were either older alcoholic men or drifters, people who kept moving from one area to another looking for work. But now all that is changing. Today the average age of the homeless is in the low thirties. And women known as bag ladies are becoming more and more familiar figures on the streets of America.

Up to half of today's homeless are former mental patients, released from state mental hospitals but with nowhere to go. Thousands more are men, women, and children who were thrown out of old tenements or cheap hotels during the seventies and eighties as cities rebuilt their downtown areas. And finally, many are school dropouts who can't get or hold a job because they have no marketable skills. Since virtually no low-income housing has been built in recent years, these people have had no place to turn but to the streets.

But the homeless are just a small part of the nation's poor. According to government figures over 14 percent of the population is below the poverty

Above: *soup kitchens, such as this one for migrant workers in a church in Florida, offer some relief from starvation in America.* Opposite: *this homeless man fills a garbage bag with warm air coming from the vent of a downtown Detroit restaurant in an attempt to keep himself warm in subzero temperatures.*

level. And the percentage is much higher for children—22 percent—and higher yet for black children—nearly 50 percent! In fact, a study by the Physician Task Force on Hunger in America found that about one out of every ten Americans is "undernourished."

Many of the elderly are also suffering economic difficulties. About 5 million men and women over the age of 65 live in poverty. Another big group consists of single-parent families in which the mother is the head of the household. There are close to 4 million such families that are unable to care for themselves.

USA for Africa gave about $4 million of the $44 million raised to help America's poor and homeless. But many complained that not enough was being done. Ken Kragen, one of the organizers of USA for Africa, said, "The most common thing I heard was, 'That's good what you're doing for Africa, but what are you doing for Americans?' It was a take-care-of-home-first attitude, and I kept hearing this in a lot of different ways."

In May 1985 Ken Kragen began thinking of a way to ease the suffering of America's needy. He wanted to raise money but also arouse compassion in the hearts of his fellow Americans. After the success of the earlier records and concerts he realized that he had to create an event that would be even more spectacular and imaginative than Live Aid.

Kragen's idea "to help Americans help Americans" was to hold the biggest get-together in our country's history. He proposed Hands Across America, a national fund-raising event for the 1986 Memorial Day weekend. "In order to make a difference, you have to do something major that captures the attention," said Kragen. "This is just impossible enough to be possible."

On Sunday, May 25, approximately six million people, almost all of whom had contributed or pledged at least $10, joined hands and formed a 4,150-mile (6,400-km) human chain stretching from coast to coast. At the head of the line in New York was six-year-old Amy Sherwood, whose family of seven had been homeless for almost one year. Near her stood Harry Belafonte, Yoko Ono and her son, New York's Governor Mario Cuomo, and other celebrities and officials. "This is the richest country in the world," said entertainer Ben Vereen from his place near the other end of the line in Long Beach, California. "There is no excuse for hunger." President Reagan, his wife Nancy, and 225 White House staff people and their families, joined hands along the north portico of the White House.

The chain wound through sixteen states, passed through five hundred

Hands Across America
participants in New York City

communities, one jail, and two deserts, and crossed ten rivers and one mountain range. The links included people of all ages, from all backgrounds and all walks of life. The sum they raised for the nation's hungry and homeless was about $20 million.

At precisely 3 P.M., Eastern Daylight Time, everyone joined in singing three songs—"America the Beautiful," "We Are the World," and a new song, "Hands Across America." This last song pointed up the key role of ordinary citizens in the fight against hunger.

"Hands Across America" was written and recorded especially for the occasion. The instrumental tracks for the recording were done by the rock band Toto, at Kenny Rogers' studio in Los Angeles. The vocals were provided by a children's choir and several solo singers. And, as with "We Are the World," all proceeds from sales of the record are going to the USA for Africa Foundation.

Celebrities Bill Cosby, Kenny Rogers, Pete Rose, and Lily Tomlin, co-chairs of the project, called Hands Across America the largest participatory event in all history. Coca Cola and other major corporations donated millions to meet the $18 million in expenses. American Express sponsored the route's "toughest mile," a stretch of barren desert in Arizona, and flew people out to fill it.

Harry Belafonte, Tina Turner, and Aretha Franklin were involved with the project from the beginning. The rock star Prince paid for a whole mile. And a number of other musicians joined the drive, including Dolly Parton, Brenda Lee, the Oak Ridge Boys, and Karen Taylor-Good.

Of the money raised by Hands Across America, 10 percent is going to emergency aid, 50 percent to fund programs that are already in existence, and 40 percent to start new programs to help the American poor.

Referring to U.S. Senator and Attorney General Robert F. Kennedy's comment that ideas are like pebbles you drop in the water from which ripples flow, Kragen said this about Hands Across America: "It is a boulder we dropped in the water. Tidal waves will come from this."

Another huge benefit to raise money for the starving of Africa took place on the same day as Hands Across America. Called Sport Aid, it was organized by Bob Geldof, the driving force behind Band Aid and Live Aid. Altogether twenty million runners in seventy-six countries took part in raising an estimated $150 million. Sport Aid is now the largest single fund-raising event in history.

A key event in Sport Aid was the lighting of a symbolic torch at the United Nations by Omar Khalifa, a champion African runner. Khalifa lit the first torch from the embers of a fire in a Sudanese relief camp. He was then flown to twelve European capitals. While running through each one, he was greeted by such leaders as Prime Minister Margaret Thatcher and Pope John Paul II.

The concern of musicians for world hunger, struggling American farmers, apartheid, and poverty at home has triggered a series of fund-raising events around the world. What is happening has been described by Joan Baez as "some kind of phenomenon." She said, "Rock 'n' rollers are answering a need of young people to make something out of ashes and silence." Many others are now following their lead.

INDEX

ABOUT THE AUTHOR

Gilda Berger is a former teacher of
special education and a writer on a
wide variety of social issues.

For Franklin Watts, she has published
critically acclaimed books on the
subjects of addiction, mental illness,
and PMS. She is currently at work on
two future projects for Watts, a book
on the drug "crack" and a book on the
legal and social issues of smoking.

Gilda is married to author and
concert musician Melvin Berger.
They live in Great Neck, New York.